D1710820

Nora the Naturalist's Animals

Pond Life

A+

Smart Apple Media

Published by Smart Apple Media, an imprint of Black Rabbit Books
P.O. Box 3263, Mankato, Minnesota 56002
www.blackrabbitbooks.com

Produced by David West ⚇ Children's Books
7 Princeton Court, 55 Felsham Road, London SW15 1AZ

Designed and illustrated by David West

Copyright © 2013 David West Children's Books

Cataloging-in-Publication data is available from the Library of Congress.
ISBN 978-1-62588-001-7 (library binding)
ISBN 978-1-62588-053-6 (paperback)

Printed in China
CPSIA compliance information: DWCB13CP
010313

9 8 7 6 5 4 3 2 1

Nora the Naturalist says:
I will tell you something
more about the animal.

Learn what this animal eats.

Where in the world is the animal found?

Its size is revealed!

What animal group is it – mammal, bird, reptile, amphibian, insect, or something else?

Interesting facts.

Contents

Broad-bodied chaser dragonfly

Nora the Naturalist says:
Dragonflies lay their eggs in ponds or on plants growing on ponds. The eggs hatch into **nymphs** which spend around three years underwater. The nymph eventually crawls up a reed and its skin splits to release the adult dragonfly.

Dragonflies eat other insects, and even small fish when they are nymphs.

Dragonflies can be found in wetlands all over the world, except in the polar regions.

The average wingspan of this dragonfly is 2.75 inches (70 mm).

Dragonflies are insects. They are not members of the true fly family.

Large dragonflies have a maximum speed of 22–34 mph (10–15 meters per second).

Dragonflies

Dragonflies are one of the fastest insect fliers. They hunt other insects such as mosquitos and flies. They spend most of their life as nymphs living underwater.

5

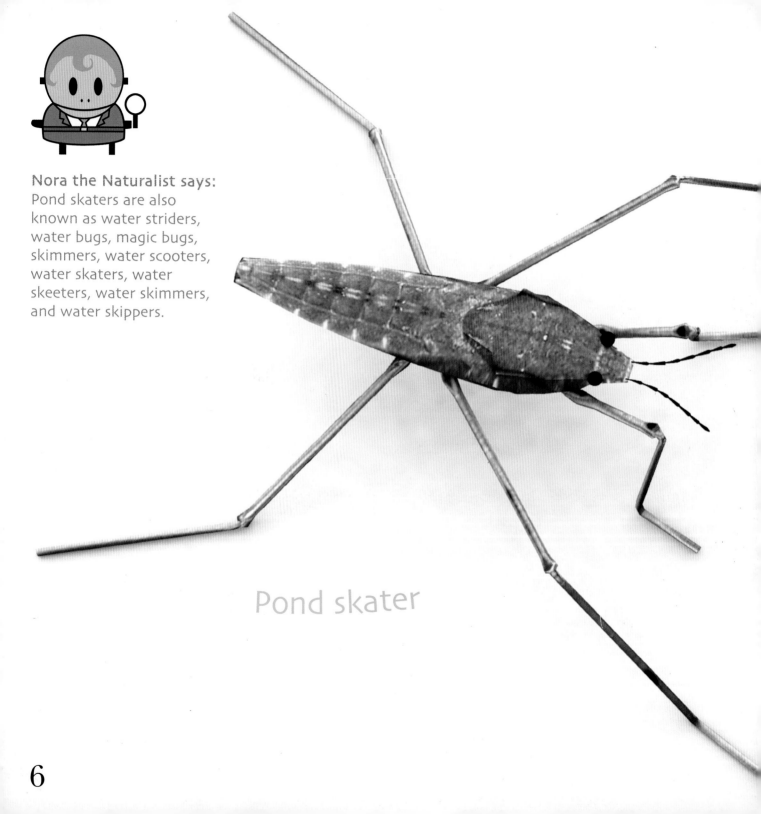

Nora the Naturalist says:
Pond skaters are also known as water striders, water bugs, magic bugs, skimmers, water scooters, water skaters, water skeeters, water skimmers, and water skippers.

Pond skater

Pond Skaters

Pond skaters can be seen on ponds, scooting across the surface. Microscopic hairs on their legs trap air bubbles that allow them to float on the water's surface. They have wings so they can fly away from water to **hibernate** during the winter.

Pond skaters feed on insects that fall into the water.

Pond skaters are found in ponds around the world in temperate or tropical climates.

Pond skaters are about 0.8 inches (20 mm) long.

Pond skaters are members of the true bugs family of insects.

Pond skaters are very agile on the surface of the water and can jump to evade predators.

Mosquitos

Mosquitos are found in warm and humid regions where there is standing water. They lay their eggs in or on the water. Only the female mosquito sucks blood from animals. They can transmit diseases such as **malaria**.

Nora the Naturalist says:
In warm regions of the world, they are active all year, but in cooler regions they hibernate in winter. Arctic mosquitos may live for only a few weeks while pools of water form on top of the **permafrost**.

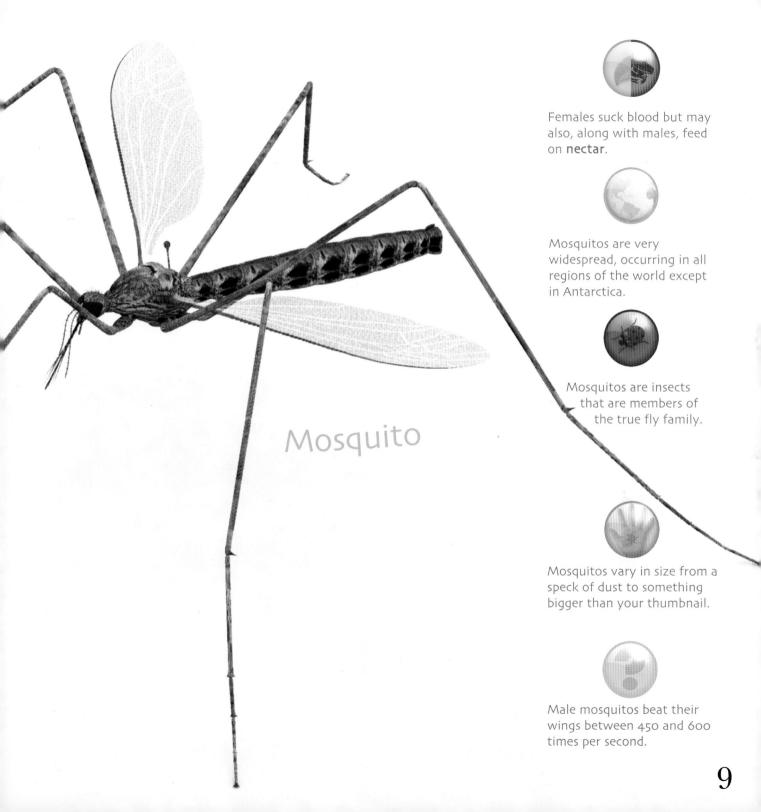

Mosquito

Females suck blood but may also, along with males, feed on **nectar**.

Mosquitos are very widespread, occurring in all regions of the world except in Antarctica.

Mosquitos are insects that are members of the true fly family.

Mosquitos vary in size from a speck of dust to something bigger than your thumbnail.

Male mosquitos beat their wings between 450 and 600 times per second.

Carp eat floating plants, algae, mosquitos, midge flies, larvae, and unlucky bugs near the water's surface, tadpoles, and small fish. They also sift through mud for worms, freshwater shrimp, and snails.

Native to central Asia, carp are the most widely distributed freshwater fish in the world.

Carp are members of the ray-finned fish family.

Carp can grow to very large sizes but koi generally grow to around 12 inches (30 cm).

Koi were originally bred in Japan in various colors and patterns.

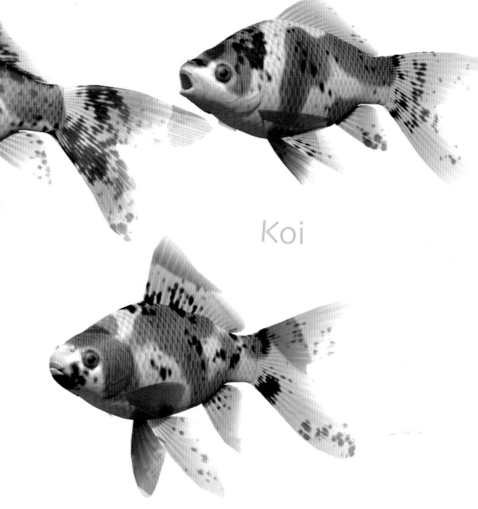

Koi

10

Carp

Various species of carp have been domesticated and raised for food in ponds across Europe and Asia for thousands of years. They have also been bred as ornamental fish for outdoor ponds.

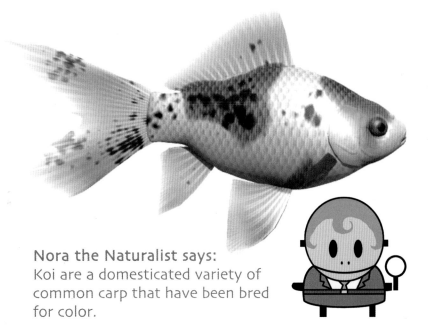

Nora the Naturalist says:
Koi are a domesticated variety of common carp that have been bred for color.

Wild Fish

Wild ponds may contain a variety of wild fish, the most common being the stickleback. The male stickleback is a very good father.

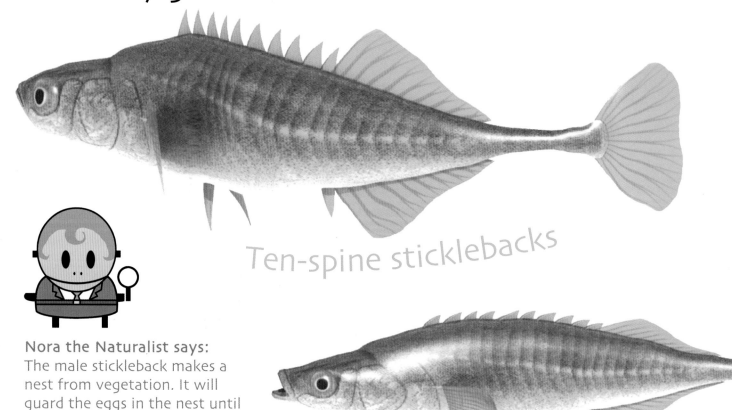

Ten-spine sticklebacks

Nora the Naturalist says:
The male stickleback makes a nest from vegetation. It will guard the eggs in the nest until they hatch.

12

Sticklebacks eat worms, insect larvae, and crustaceans.

 Sticklebacks live in fresh water and saltwater and are common in mild northern climates around the world, including Europe, North America, Asia, and Japan.

 Their maximum length is about 4 inches (10 cm), but few of them grow to more than 3 inches (8 cm) long.

 Sticklebacks are members of the ray-finned fish family.

 They are also known as burnstickle, common stickleback, European stickleback, jacksharp, and tiddler.

Turtles

In some parts of the world, freshwater turtles can be found living in and around ponds. These shy animals are good swimmers. They hunt for various types of water creatures and feed on plants.

Nora the Naturalist says:
Red-eared sliders get their name from the red patch of skin on their neck and their ability to slide off rocks into the water quickly.

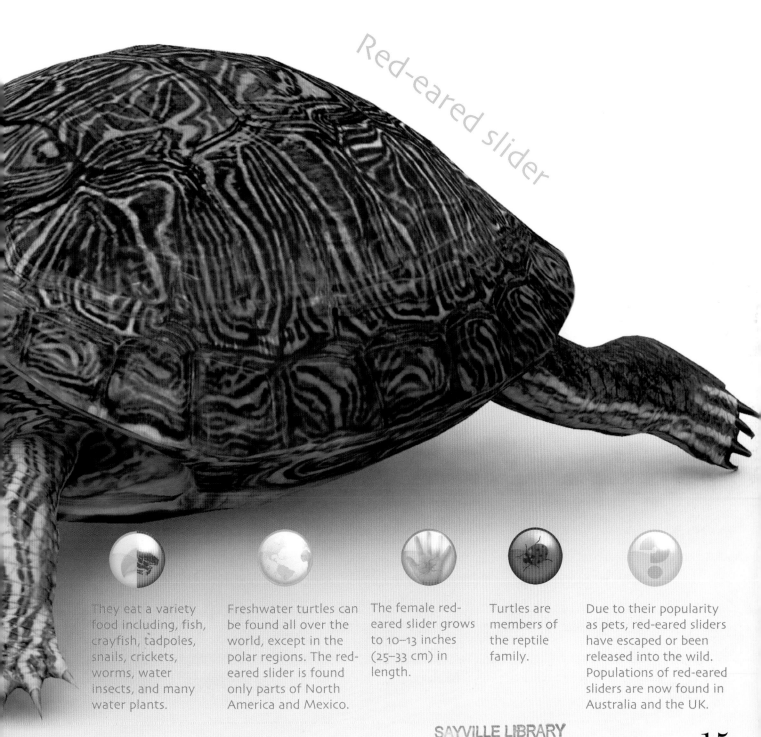

Red-eared slider

They eat a variety food including, fish, crayfish, tadpoles, snails, crickets, worms, water insects, and many water plants.

Freshwater turtles can be found all over the world, except in the polar regions. The red-eared slider is found only parts of North America and Mexico.

The female red-eared slider grows to 10–13 inches (25–33 cm) in length.

Turtles are members of the reptile family.

Due to their popularity as pets, red-eared sliders have escaped or been released into the wild. Populations of red-eared sliders are now found in Australia and the UK.

15

Frogs

Frogs are amphibians, so they can live on land and in water. Frogs start life as tadpoles after hatching from frogspawn. Eventually they lose their tail and gills and become air-breathing frogs.

Nora the Naturalist says:
Frogs can catch flies on their long, sticky tongues.

Common frog

Favorite foods include insects, snails, slugs, and worms.

Frogs are found on all the continents except Antarctica but they are not present on certain islands, especially those far away from large areas of land.

Frogs are amphibians.

Adult common frogs have a body length of 2.4 to 3.5 inches (6 to 9 cm).

Some frogs, such as the poison dart frogs, are very poisonous.

Toads

Toads are like frogs. They lay their eggs in ponds. After changing into an adult toad, they spend most of their life on land. They have warty-looking skin which helps them blend into their surroundings.

Nora the Naturalist says:
Toads give off a poison from skin glands when they are disturbed. This stops most predators from eating them.

American toad

Their diet includes crickets, worms, ants, spiders, slugs, centipedes, moths, and other small insects.

Toads are widespread and occur on every continent except Antarctica.

Toads are members of the amphibian family.

The American toad is a medium-sized toad around 1.9–3.5 inches (5–9 cm) in length.

Some toads, like the American toad, hibernate during winter.

Newts

Newts hatch from eggs in a pond and go through a change from tadpole to juvenile. The juveniles leave the pond to grow into adults. Then they either return to live in the water for the rest of their lives, or live on land, returning to the water each year to lay eggs.

Nora the Naturalist says:
When the juvenile newt leaves the water and lives on land it is called an eft.

Red-spotted newt

Newts eat insects, snails, crustaceans, young amphibians, frogs' eggs, and worms.

Newts are found in North America, Europe, the Middle East, Southeast Asia, and Japan.

Newts are amphibians that are members of the salamander family.

Many newts produce poisons from their skin as a defense against predators.

The red spotted newt may grow to 5 inches (12.5 cm) in length.

21

Herons prey on fish, frogs, and other small water animals.

Herons can be found on every continent in the world except Antarctica.

Herons are members of the bird family.

Herons vary in size from 17–60 inches (44–152 cm) or more in length.

Herons have long legs so that they can wade in the water without getting their feathers wet.

Gray heron

Purple heron

Herons

Ponds around the world may get occasional visits from a heron. These patient birds hunt for fish and other small water animals in shallow water.

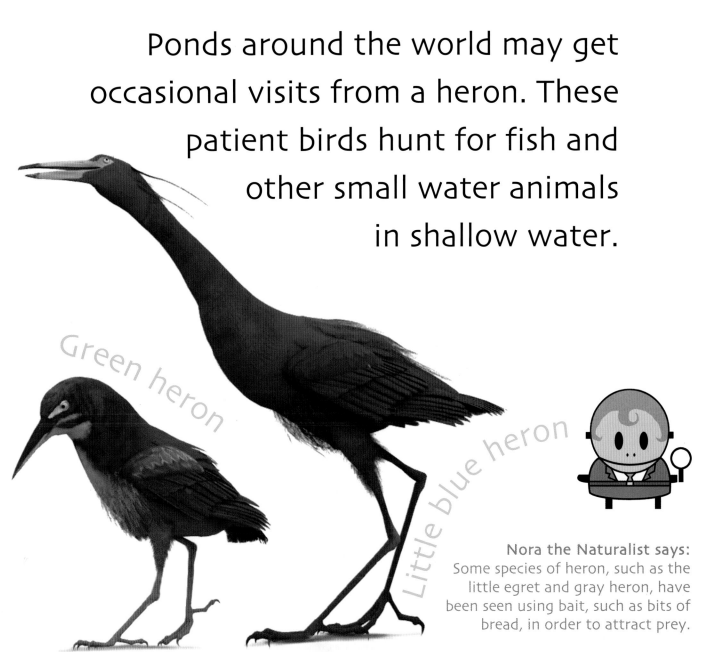

Green heron

Little blue heron

Nora the Naturalist says: Some species of heron, such as the little egret and gray heron, have been seen using bait, such as bits of bread, in order to attract prey.

Glossary

hibernate
To spend winter in a sleeping state.

malaria
A disease of humans and other animals, transmitted by mosquitos.

nectar
A sweet liquid secreted by the flowers of various plants, and drunk by hummingbirds and insects.

nymph
A water-living stage of an insect before it becomes an adult.

permafrost
Soil that is frozen.

Index